D1442550

THE ELEMENTS

Molybdenum

Nathan Lepora

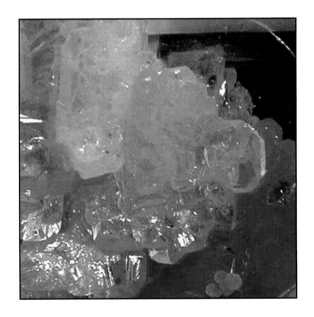

Marshall Cavendish
Benchmark

New York

Marshall Cavendish Benchmark
99 White Plains Road
Tarrytown, New York 10591

www.marshallcavendish.us

Library of Congress Cataloging-in-Publication Data

Lepora, Nathan.
Molybdenum / Nathan Lepora.
p.   cm. — (The elements)
Includes index.
ISBN-13: 978-0-7614-2201-3
ISBN-10: 0-7614-2201-3
1. Molybdenum—Juvenile literature.
I. Title. II. Elements (Marshall Cavendish Benchmark)

QD181.M7L47 2006
546'.534—dc22

2005057096

1 6 5 4 3 2

Printed in Malaysia

Picture credits
Front cover: 2004 RGB Research Ltd
Back cover: Corbis

2004 RGB Research Ltd: www.element-collection.com 4
Stan Celestian: 1, 12
Corbis: 16, Brownie Harris 22, Robert Pickett 25, Roger Ressmeyer 6, David H. Wells 14
Corbis Royalty Free: 23
Getty Images: 10
NASA: 30, JPL 13
Photos.com: 3, 5, 20
Science & Society Picture Library: Science Museum 9
Science Photo Library: Martin Bond 24, Dr. Jeremy Burgess 19, Russ Lappa 8, Astrid & Hans Frieder Michler 17
University of Pennsylvania Library: Edgar Fahs Smith Collection 11
U.S. Air Force: 7

Series created by The Brown Reference Group plc.
Designed by Sarah Williams
www.brownreference.com

Contents

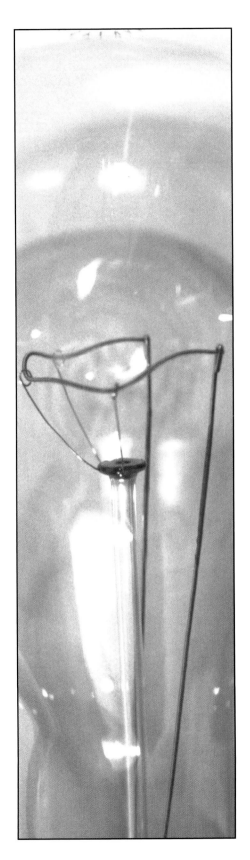

What is molybdenum?

Molybdenum is a rare, silvery white metal with an extremely high melting point. It is commonly used in wire supports holding the glowing filament in light bulbs. Molybdenum is also an ingredient in some stainless steels and in "superalloys" for jet and rocket engines. Chemicals containing molybdenum are used in some paints and dyes and for making fireproof materials.

In nature, plants need tiny amounts of molybdenum from the soil to thrive. Nothing can grow naturally in soil that does not contain any molybdenum. Animals also use small amounts of this element in some of the chemical reactions that take place in their bodies.

Pure molybdenum metal does not exist in nature. When it has been purified, molybdenum is a very tough metal that does not melt easily.

The molybdenum atom

Everything is made of many tiny particles called atoms. These atoms are incredibly small. One speck of dust contains more atoms than the number of grains of sand on a beach.

Solid substances, such as molybdenum, have their atoms stacked closely together. If a substance contains only one type of atom then it is called an element. There are about ninety different elements found on Earth. Most elements are metals like molybdenum, but some are nonmetals, such as hydrogen, sulfur, or oxygen.

Elements bind together chemically to make new substances called compounds. Compounds are often very different from the elements that form them.

Inside the atom

Even though atoms are very tiny, they are made of even smaller particles called protons, neutrons, and electrons. The protons and neutrons clump together in a central core called the nucleus. The electrons circle around this nucleus, similar to the way the planets orbit the Sun. These electrons form layers, or shells, around the nucleus.

Internal forces

Every proton has a positive charge and every electron has a negative charge. Opposite charges attract each other, so the electrons are pulled toward the protons and circle the nucleus.

Atoms are neutral—they have no overall charge. This is because the number of an atom's electrons equals the number of its

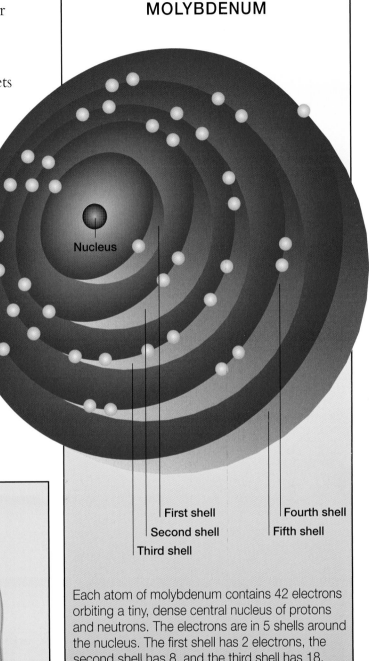

MOLYBDENUM

Nucleus

First shell
Second shell
Third shell

Fourth shell
Fifth shell

Each atom of molybdenum contains 42 electrons orbiting a tiny, dense central nucleus of protons and neutrons. The electrons are in 5 shells around the nucleus. The first shell has 2 electrons, the second shell has 8, and the third shell has 18. The outer 2 shells are incomplete. The fourth shell has 13 of its 18 spaces filled, while the fifth and outermost shell has 1 of 8 spaces occupied.

The main use of molybdenum is in heat-resistant components of light bulbs.

A view inside an electric vacuum oven. The oven is used to make things very hot without burning them. The furnace is lined with heat-resistant molybdenum.

protons. The negative and positive charges cancel each other out. During chemical reactions, some atoms lose or gain electrons. This gives them a positive or negative charge, and they become ions.

Atomic numbers

A molybdenum nucleus always contains 42 protons. This number is called the atomic number. Each element has a unique atomic number. For example, hydrogen's atomic number is 1, carbon's is 12, and iron's is 26. Atoms are also identified by their atomic mass number. This counts an atom's total number of protons and neutrons. Molybdenum has an atomic mass number of 96. This means that each molybdenum atom has an average of 54 neutrons and 42 protons.

A transition metal

Chemistry is the study of how elements form compounds. An element's chemical properties depend on the element's atomic number. This is because chemical bonds are formed by atoms taking, giving, or sharing electrons. The number of electrons in the outermost shell determines how many electrons the atom can take, share, or give away. Molybdenum has a complicated chemistry because it uses two outer shells for chemical reactions.

A family of elements, called the transition elements, uses two outer electron shells in reactions. These elements are all metals. Most are hard and do not melt easily. Transition metals have many useful properties. They do not react easily. This makes them good for making long-lasting materials and protective coatings. Transition metal compounds often have bright colors, so they make good paints and dyes. Atoms of transition metals also mix well to form alloys (mixtures of metals). For example, steel is an alloy of iron and other transition metals. Molybdenum is a typical transition metal. Others include chromium, tungsten, and iron.

A missile is launched into the sky using a rocket engine. The engine gets very hot and contains molybdenum to prevent it from melting.

Special characteristics

Molybdenum is a very hard metal and will not bend out of shape easily. The metal stays hard even at very high temperatures that would melt most other metals.

Molybdenum's other physical properties are similar to those of chromium (Cr) and tungsten (W), the two metals lying directly above and below molybdenum in the periodic table.

Inside solids

All substances can exist as a solid, liquid, or gas. In solids, the atoms are held together in a rigid shape. Solid metals, including molybdenum, have atoms closely stacked together in an ordered repeating pattern. Between these atoms, the outermost electrons escape into a freely flowing "sea" of electrons. The atoms' nuclei are strongly attracted to this negatively charged electron sea. The result is a powerful "glue" that bonds the metal atoms rigidly together.

Melting point

Heat causes atoms to vibrate. The atoms in a solid vibrate more as the temperature increases. When the temperature reaches that solid's melting point, the atoms have enough energy to break free of the bonds holding them together. The atoms can then slip over each other, and the substance becomes a liquid.

Molybdenum has the fifth-highest melting point of all metals, and melts at 4753 °F (2623 °C). That is almost twice as hot as steel's and even higher than the melting points of many rocks. Only tantalum, rhenium, osmium, and tungsten melt at higher temperatures. Tungsten has the highest melting point of all metals.

Molybdenum's high melting point makes it useful for making heating elements and other components that get very hot. However, the metal's hardness makes it difficult to bend into shapes.

MOLYBDENUM FACTS

- Chemical symbol — Mo
- Atomic number — 42
- Atomic weight — 95.94
- Melting point — 4753 °F (2623 °C)
- Boiling point — 8382 °F (4639 °C)
- Density — 10.2 grams per cubic centimeter (10.2 times that of water)

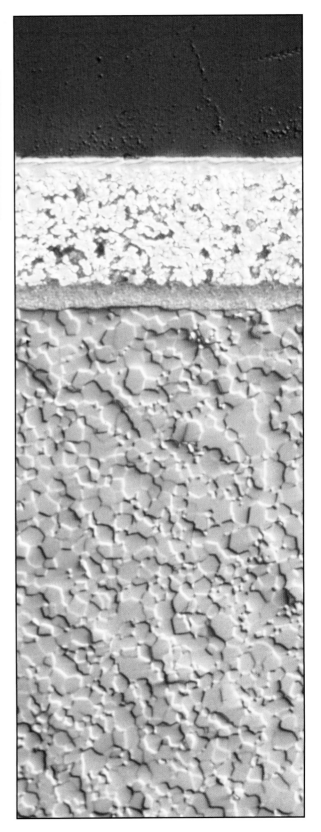

Electron sea

The electron "glue" in molybdenum is especially strong, which is why it has such a high melting point. The other metals have higher melting points because their atoms are twice as heavy as molybdenum's. The heavy atoms need more energy to break free of the electron "glue."

The electron "sea" also creates other metallic properties. For example, electricity is a flow of electrons through a substance. All metals conduct electricity well because of their free electrons. These free electrons also carry heat energy, making metals good heat conductors. This is why a metal spoon becomes hotter faster than a wooden or plastic one, when it is left in a hot drink.

A close-up of a cross section of a piece of pottery that has been magnified 200 times. The yellow clay is coated with an alloy of tin and gold, which gives it a shiny surface. The coating is held in place by a thin layer of molybdenum, shown here in green. The molybdenum stops the coating from breaking off.

The history of molybdenum

The most common natural form of molybdenum is a mineral called molybdenite. Scientists first separated pure molybdenum metal from molybdenite in the late eighteenth century. Before that time, they thought molybdenite was just another lead-based rock. This idea began with the ancient Greeks, who believed lead, graphite carbon, galena (a gray lead-containing mineral), and molybdenite were all the same material, called molybdos.

Japanese sword makers were using molybdenum hundreds of years ago. Recent analysis of a fourteenth-century Samurai sword found molybdenum in the steel. It is a mystery how the swordsmith made this alloy.

Molybdenum's discovery

In late 1777 the Swedish pharmacist Carl Wilhelm Scheele asked other European chemists for samples of molybdenite.

A metal fortress made by French steelmakers on show at the Paris Exhibition in 1900. The fortress was strengthened with molybdenum alloys.

Carl Wilhelm Scheele discovered a total of six elements: chlorine, barium, tungsten, molybdenum, nitrogen, and manganese.

At the time, scientists thought molybdenite was a lead mineral, and were not very interested in it. That changed a few months later when Scheele announced that molybdenite contained a new element combined with sulfur.

Scheele tried to extract the pure metal but did not succeed. His best effort was to make powdery white molybdenum trioxide (MoO_3). In 1782 Scheele's friend Peter Jacob Hjelm (1746-1813) finally managed to purify the metal. Hjelm heated Scheele's white powder with carbon, which pulled away the oxygen atoms to leave pure molybdenum behind.

Wartime molybdenum

Molybdenum was not widely used until World War I (1914–1918). At the time, there was not enough tungsten to mix with steel to make hard armor plates. Scientists found that molybdenum was a good alternative. The immense German artillery gun "Big Bertha" was made of molybdenum-hardened steel. Molybdenum is still used to make armor for tanks and other military machines.

By 1918 the world's largest molybdenum mine was working near Climax, Colorado. The United States still produces the most molybdenum today.

Where molybdenum is found

On Earth, natural molybdenum is found only combined with other elements. Its most common natural compound is molybdenum disulfide (MoS_2). This has two atoms of sulfur bound to every atom of molybdenum. Molybdenum disulfide forms naturally as the mineral molybdenite. Molybdenite is buried deep underground in rocks.

Scientists estimate that the rocks in Earth's crust contain about 0.0001 percent molybdenum. This is far less than common

Molybdenite is the main source of molybdenum. Most molybdenite comes from the western United States, Chile, and China.

metals like copper and chromium, but still more than precious metals, such as silver and gold.

Rocks, minerals, and ores

Minerals are natural chemical compounds that usually form as crystals. Ores are the rocks that contain a lot of valuable elements, such as metals. All rocks, including ores, are made of mixtures of minerals. Some precious metals, such as silver and gold, are found as pure metal mixed up with

Wulfenite is a mineral that contains equal amounts of lead and molybdenum. With both these heavy metals in it, wulfenite is very dense.

A Russian space probe found pure molybdenum on the Moon. Pure molybdenum has never been found on Earth.

other minerals. Most other metal ores are made of compounds containing oxygen (oxides) or sulfur (sulfides).

Molybdenite is a sulfide ore and molybdenum's most natural ore. It is metallic gray, feels slippery, and is soft and flaky. Molybdenite forms deep underground when certain kinds of lavas (melted minerals) cool into rock.

Wulfenite is another mineral containing molybdenum. It is a compound of lead, molybdenum, and oxygen and has the chemical name lead molybdate ($PbMoO_2$). Wulfenite is much rarer than molybdenite and not very useful as an ore.

Crystals of wulfenite are a mixture of bright orange, red, and yellow fragments. Some crystals are large chunks, while others are thin see-through flakes.

Molybdenum in nature
Most plants and animals need a tiny amount of molybdenum to stay healthy. The molybdenum becomes part of an enzyme, which is a substance that takes part in the chemical reactions needed for life. A lack of molybdenum will kill plants.

People usually eat a tiny amount (about 0.01 milligram) of molybdenum in their food each day. This mostly comes from the vegetables they eat, and totals almost 0.3 grams over a whole lifetime. Even so, only about 5 milligrams of molybdenum can be stored in the body at one time.

Mining and refining

A molybdenum ore mine in New Mexico is extracting wulfenite using the open-pit method.

Almost all molybdenum is mined as the mineral molybdenite. Some mines also extract wulfenite. Huge reserves of molybdenum ores are buried underneath the mountains of North and South America. In 2004, 139,000 tons (126,100 tonnes) of molybdenum ore was mined. This was worth more than a billion dollars.

MOLYBDENUM FACTS

About 140,000 tons (127,000 tonnes) of molybdenum ore are mined each year. The total known deposits of molybdenum are about 20 million tons (18 million tonnes). This is enough to last another 150 years. The world's leading producers of molybdenum in 2004 were

	Mined	Reserves
United States	39,900 tons (35,900 tonnes)	5,400,000 tons (4,860,000 tonnes)
Chile	33,400 tons (30,000 tonnes)	2,500,000 tons (2,250,000 tonnes)
China	31,000 tons (27,900 tonnes)	8,300,000 tons (7,470,000 tonnes)
Peru	11,000 tons (9,900 tonnes)	230,000 tons (207,000 tonnes)
Canada	9,700 tons (8,730 tonnes)	910,000 tons (820,000 tonnes)
Others	14,000 tons (12,600 tonnes)	1,660,000 tons (1,500,000 tonnes)

Mining and separation

Molybdenum ore is found mixed with other rocks. This means that miners must remove massive quantities of material to reach the valuable mineral. One way to mine molybdenum is to dig a huge hole, or pit. This is the open-pit method. Often the side of a mountain is dug away to reach the ore. Another method is underground block caving. Miners dig under large blocks of ore, which collapse into huge caverns.

Once on the surface, the ore is prepared for processing. At milling plants, the mined ore is crushed into dust. Huge rotating balls and gigantic crushers grind the ore into a fine mixture of tiny molybdenite particles and powdered rock.

Huge flotation tanks are then used to separate the valuable ore from worthless rock. The powdery mixture is first mixed with water, and air is bubbled through the thin porridge-like slurry. Powdered molybdenite sticks to bubbles, which float to the top of the tank. Skimming off this froth then separates the concentrated ore from everything else.

Roasting

Most industries do not want the sulfur in the molybdenite. Instead, factories convert the powdered molybdenite into molybdenum trioxide (MoO_2), also known as tech oxide.

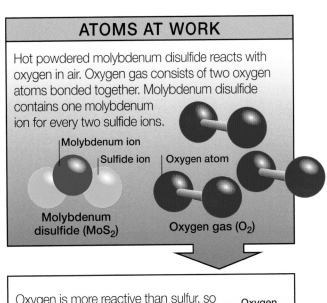

ATOMS AT WORK

Hot powdered molybdenum disulfide reacts with oxygen in air. Oxygen gas consists of two oxygen atoms bonded together. Molybdenum disulfide contains one molybdenum ion for every two sulfide ions.

Molybdenum ion

Sulfide ion

Oxygen atom

Molybdenum disulfide (MoS_2)

Oxygen gas (O_2)

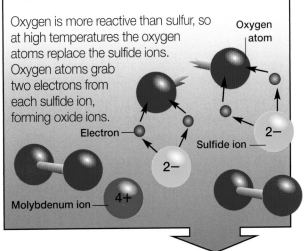

Oxygen is more reactive than sulfur, so at high temperatures the oxygen atoms replace the sulfide ions. Oxygen atoms grab two electrons from each sulfide ion, forming oxide ions.

Oxygen atom

Electron

Sulfide ion

2−

2−

Molybdenum ion

4+

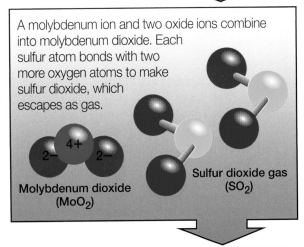

A molybdenum ion and two oxide ions combine into molybdenum dioxide. Each sulfur atom bonds with two more oxygen atoms to make sulfur dioxide, which escapes as gas.

4+

2−

2−

Molybdenum dioxide (MoO_2)

Sulfur dioxide gas (SO_2)

The reaction that takes place can be written like this:

$$MoS_2 + 3O_2 \rightarrow MoO_2 + 2SO_2$$

ATOMS AT WORK

Oxygen reacts with hot molybdenum dioxide formed from roasting molybdenite. During the reaction, the bond between another pair of oxygen atoms breaks apart.

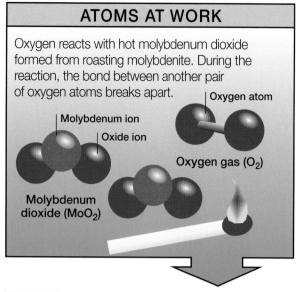

Oxygen atom

Molybdenum ion

Oxide ion

Oxygen gas (O_2)

Molybdenum dioxide (MoO_2)

One of these oxygen atoms becomes an oxide ion by grabbing two electrons from the molybdenum ion.

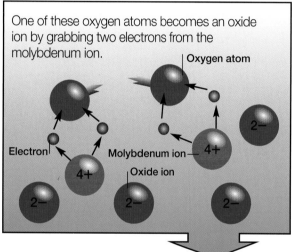

Oxygen atom

Electron

Molybdenum ion

Oxide ion

This oxide ion then binds to the molybdenum dioxide, making molybdenum trioxide.

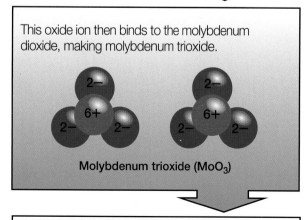

Molybdenum trioxide (MoO_3)

The reaction that takes place can be written like this:

$$2MoO_2 + O_2 \rightarrow 2MoO_3$$

The most common way of making tech oxide is to roast molybdenite. Roasting typically takes ten hours at temperatures of 1112 °F (600 °C). Molybdenite burns in air, giving off heat, so water sprays are used to stop the furnaces from overheating. The reaction happens in two steps. First, oxygen atoms exchange places with the sulfur atoms, making molybdenum dioxide (MoO_2). Then another oxygen atom attaches to make molybdenum trioxide (MoO_3).

The tech oxide is finally shaped into pillow-shaped bricks or drums of powder. It is sold to steelworks, other metal producers, and to the chemical industry.

Rocks rich in molybdenite near the Rocky-Mountain ghost town of Climax, Colorado. This is part of the world's largest source of molybdenum ore.

Metal production

Pure molybdenum metal is a key ingredient for many industries. However, mining and refining plants produce tech oxide (molybdenum trioxide; MoO_3), not the pure metal. Before it can be used, the molybdenum needs to be separated from the tech oxide. This type of reaction is called smelting.

Ferromolybdenum

Pure molybdenum is used for very specialized objects such as rocket-engine nozzles, but it is more common to use molybdenum mixed with iron. This alloy is called ferromolybdenum (FeMo). It is an essential ingredient for an extremely tough steel, known as "moly."

Smelting

Smelting makes ferromolybdenum from iron and molybdenum trioxide. It does this with the help of a reactive metal like powdered aluminum. Igniting the mixture starts the reaction, which fizzes and fumes violently. The aluminum atoms grab the oxide ions from the

A close-up view of the crystals inside a piece of aluminum and molybdenum alloy. This alloy is used to coat other metal objects to protect them from corrosion. The metal has been magnified 125 times.

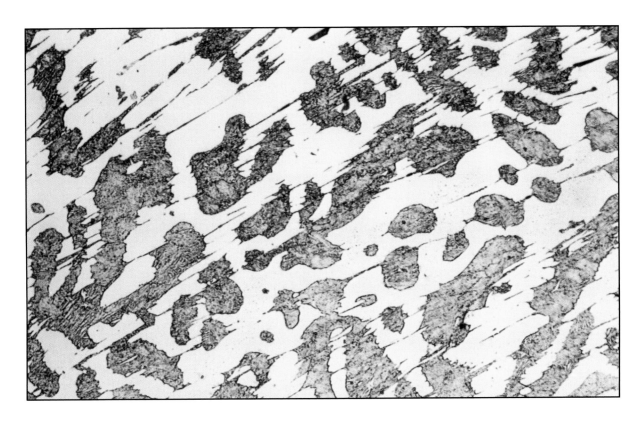

ATOMS AT WORK

Hot hydrogen reacts with molybdenum trioxide to make a pure metal. Hydrogen gas consists of two hydrogen atoms bonded together. Crystals of molybdenum trioxide contain one molybdenum ion for every three oxide ions.

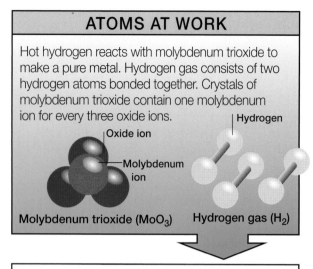

Oxide ion

Hydrogen

Molybdenum ion

Molybdenum trioxide (MoO₃)   Hydrogen gas (H₂)

During the reaction, the chemical bonds between three pairs of hydrogen atoms break apart. Meanwhile, each oxide ion loses two electrons to the molybdenum ion to become an oxygen atom.

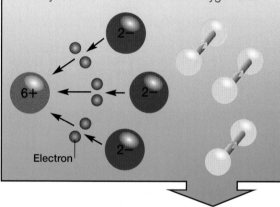

2−

6+   2−

2−

Electron

Two hydrogen atoms bond with each oxygen atom to make water. This leaves behind just the molybdenum atom as a pure metal.

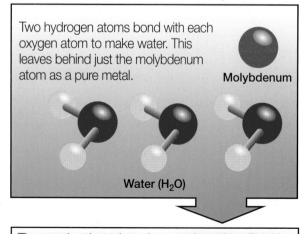

Molybdenum

Water (H₂O)

The reaction that takes place can be written like this:

$$MoO_3 + 3H_2 \rightarrow Mo + 3H_2O$$

molybdenum ions to leave a molten mix of iron, molybdenum, and aluminum oxide (Al_2O_3). This type of smelting reaction is also called the thermite process. After the mixture cools, the brittle aluminum oxide can be broken off to leave pure ferromolybdenum.

Molybdenum metal

Smelting can also be used to extract pure molybdenum from molybdenum trioxide. Instead of aluminum, hot hydrogen gas is used to remove the oxygen from the metal oxide. As a result, pure molybdenum is left behind.

The reactive hydrogen atoms grab the oxide ions from the molybdenum ions. This reaction forms the very common and familiar compound of hydrogen and oxygen known as water (H_2O). Pure molybdenum is left behind.

Powder

Molybdenum does not melt until it reaches very high temperatures. This makes it difficult to mold the metal into bars or other useful shapes. Instead, it is easier to produce pure molybdenum as a fine powder. The powder is poured into molds and is then melted to turn it into a single, solid structure. This is done by passing a huge electric current through the powder, which makes the tiny grains of metal fuse together.

Chemistry and compounds

Molybdenum disulfide is a slippery substance. It is sprayed onto objects to stop them from getting scratched. This is a magnified view of the scratches in the layer of molybdenum disulfide. However, the surface underneath is not damaged.

Like all metals, molybdenum can react and form compounds with nonmetals. It does this by losing its outermost electrons. Chemists call this process a redox reaction. *Redox* is short for "reduction and oxidation." Oxidation occurs when metal atoms lose electrons to make positively charged ions. The opposite process, reduction, is when nonmetal atoms gain electrons to make negatively charged ions.

Range of charges

A characteristic property of transition metals is that they can form ions that have a range of charges. They do this by losing different numbers of electrons during chemical reactions. Non-transition elements always give away a fixed number of electrons. For example, sodium atoms lose one electron to make Na^+

ions, and oxygen atoms gain two electrons to make O^{2-} ions. However, molybdenum atoms can lose between two and six electrons to make Mo^{2+}, Mo^{3+}, Mo^{4+}, Mo^{5+}, and Mo^{6+} ions.

Molybdenum ions

A simple example of a redox reaction is the combination of molybdenum with oxygen from the air to make molybdenum

oxide. This reaction is very similar to the one that results in iron objects rusting, where the metal turns into crumbly red-brown iron oxide (Fe_2O_3) crystals. However, molybdenum is less reactive than iron. It takes a lot of heat energy to make molybdenum react with oxygen. Molybdenum must usually be red hot before it starts reacting with oxygen (or anything else).

Molybdenum and oxygen react in several ways to make hard white crystals. The most common reactions are when molybdenum atoms lose four or six electrons and forms Mo^{4+} or Mo^{6+} ions.

The tungsten filament of a lightbulb—the part that glows to produce the light—gets very hot. It is held in place by tiny supports made from pure molybdenum. Although they are very thin, these supports do not melt when the filament heats up.

The Mo^{4+} ions combine with two oxide (O^{2-}) ions to make molybdenum dioxide (MoO_2), while the Mo^{6+} ions bond to three oxide ions to form molybdenum trioxide (MoO_3). Molybdenum dioxide crystals also burn in air to make molybdenum trioxide.

Balancing redox reactions

Chemists know a simple way to calculate the numbers of different ions that take part in a chemical reaction. In any chemical compound, the total number of positive charges must equal the total number of negative charges. This is because chemical compounds are always neutral, so all the charges of the ions in them must balance.

A good example is how Mo^{6+} ions bond to oxide ions. Each oxide ion has charge of -2, and the molybdenum ion has charge of $+6$. The only way to balance the positive and negative charges is to have three oxide ions for every Mo^{6+} ion. This is because three -2 charges add up to be equal and opposite to one $+6$ charge.

The balancing method also works with other ions. For example, chloride ions (Cl^-) have only one negative charge. Four chloride ions are therefore needed to bond with every Mo^{4+} ion to make molybdenum tetrachloride ($MoCl_4$). To make this substance, a chemist leaves a piece of molybdenum metal in a jar of chlorine gas.

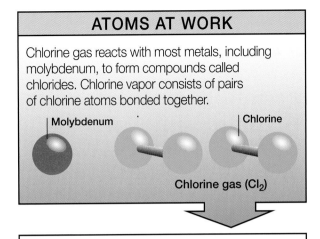

ATOMS AT WORK

Chlorine gas reacts with most metals, including molybdenum, to form compounds called chlorides. Chlorine vapor consists of pairs of chlorine atoms bonded together.

Molybdenum

Chlorine

Chlorine gas (Cl_2)

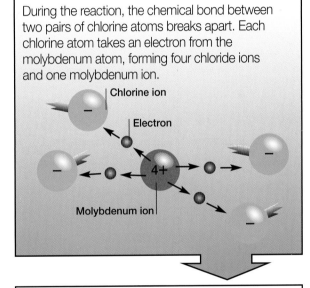

During the reaction, the chemical bond between two pairs of chlorine atoms breaks apart. Each chlorine atom takes an electron from the molybdenum atom, forming four chloride ions and one molybdenum ion.

Chlorine ion

Electron

Molybdenum ion

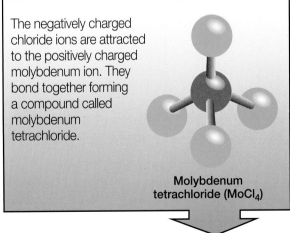

The negatively charged chloride ions are attracted to the positively charged molybdenum ion. They bond together forming a compound called molybdenum tetrachloride.

Molybdenum tetrachloride ($MoCl_4$)

The reaction that takes place can be written like this:

$Mo + 2Cl_2 \rightarrow MoCl_4$

Uses of molybdenum

Even though molybdenum metal is incredibly hard and unaffected by heat, it is too expensive to use in large amounts. The most common items containing pure molybdenum are the thin wires supports in electric light bulbs. Pure molybdenum is used to make many other specialized objects that also get very hot, such as the heating elements of electric furnaces.

However, most molybdenum metal is used as an ingredient for ultra-tough steels and other alloys. Some molybdenum is also used by the chemical industry, especially to make paints and dyes.

Molybdenum chemicals

One important molybdenum compound is the pigment molybdenum orange. This is a colored substance made mainly of lead molybdate ($PbMoO_4$). Other chemicals are mixed in to make substances that can be colored a bright yellow and blood red.

Another mass-produced molybdenum chemical, molybdenum trioxide (MoO_3), helps stop smoke from forming. For instance, it is mixed with plastics to prevent deadly fumes from being produced if the plastics catch fire. The compound is also used in the carpets and seat cushions inside trains, airplanes, and buses.

Molybdenum is one of the ingredients in the alloys used to make turbine blades. These alloys need to be tough because the fanlike turbines spin around at high speeds and get very hot.

Steels and alloys

By far the most common use of molybdenum is for making metal alloys. Adding only a small amount of

USES OF MOLYBDENUM

Mined molybdenum is mostly used for steel and alloy manufacturing, with a small amount going to the chemical industry.

Pure metal	5 percent
Chemical industry	15 percent
Tool steels	10 percent
Stainless steels	25 percent
High-strength steels	30 percent
Other steels and alloys	15 percent

everything from automobiles to oil refineries. Stainless and heat-resistant steels contain between 0.5 and 3 percent molybdenum. These alloys are used to handle hot or corrosive chemicals, such as acids. Tool steels that have between 5 and 8 percent molybdenum are used in high-speed cutting machinery and extra tough drills and presses, which may get very hot as they are used.

molybdenum can greatly change a metal's properties. The molybdenum gives its properties, such as high melting point and unreactivity, to the mixture.

The most important alloy is steel. For centuries, steel has been used for making strong machines and structures. Normal steel is a mixture of iron and small amounts of carbon. These elements combine to make a strong, hard, and flexible material. Steel is much tougher than pure iron, which is hard but brittle and shatters easily.

Steels with around 0.5 percent molybdenum are called high-strength steels. These alloys are used to make

Tough molybdenum alloys are used to make drills. This large drill is cutting down through rock to an oil field. The drill needs to be hard so it does not wear away. As it cuts, the drill gets very hot. The molybdenum in the drill keeps it from melting.

Radioactive molybdenum

Atoms of an element are not all exactly the same. The different types of atoms are called isotopes. Isotopes all have the same number of protons and electrons as each other, but they have different numbers of neutrons in the nucleus. So isotopes act in the same way during chemical reactions, but have different atomic mass numbers. Natural molybdenum metal is a mixture of seven isotopes.

Some isotopes are not very stable and break up, or decay, into other elements. Scientists call this process radioactivity. As an atom decays, high-speed particles and energy shoot out from the nucleus. This is called radiation.

Radioactive decay can happen very quickly and cause immense explosions, as in a nuclear bomb. Most radioactive isotopes, including those of molybdenum, decay slowly and produce small amounts of radiation. All radioactive materials must always be handled carefully because even tiny amounts of radiation can cause illness.

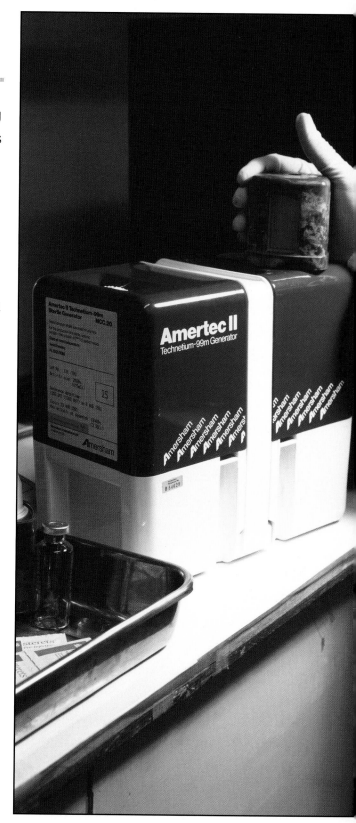

A container of molybdenum-99 in a hospital. This isotope decays into technetium, which is injected into patients during medical examinations. The radiation given off by technetium helps doctors to picture the inside of the body.

Nuclear decay

Molybdenum atoms have 42 protons, and the stable isotopes have between 50 and 58 neutrons. Artificial molybdenum isotopes are radioactive, including molybdenum-99 (Mo 99). This isotope has 42 neutrons and 47 neutrons. When Mo 99 decays, a neutron in the nucleus splits apart and forms a proton and an electron. The number of protons in the nucleus then increases by one. This changes the atom's atomic number, and so a new element is formed. When Mo 99 decays it turns into technetium. Technetium is a very rare and unstable element with an atomic number of 43—one more than molybdenum.

Medical uses

Nuclear medicine uses radioactive elements to diagnose illnesses and destroy diseased parts of the body. Doctors use cameras that detect radiation instead of light to look inside the human body. They first inject patients with a liquid containing a radioactive isotope (often technetium). The isotope gives off rays that pass through skin and other body parts.

However, technetium cannot be stored in hospitals because it decays too quickly and would soon run out. Instead molybdenum-99 is stored in hospitals. This decays more slowly and produces a steady supply of technetium, which can be used by doctors when they need it.

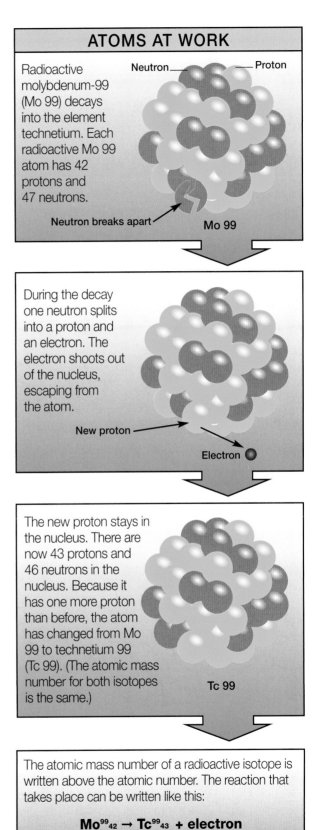

ATOMS AT WORK

Radioactive molybdenum-99 (Mo 99) decays into the element technetium. Each radioactive Mo 99 atom has 42 protons and 47 neutrons.

Neutron breaks apart — Mo 99

During the decay one neutron splits into a proton and an electron. The electron shoots out of the nucleus, escaping from the atom.

New proton — Electron

The new proton stays in the nucleus. There are now 43 protons and 46 neutrons in the nucleus. Because it has one more proton than before, the atom has changed from Mo 99 to technetium 99 (Tc 99). (The atomic mass number for both isotopes is the same.)

Tc 99

The atomic mass number of a radioactive isotope is written above the atomic number. The reaction that takes place can be written like this:

$$Mo^{99}{}_{42} \rightarrow Tc^{99}{}_{43} + electron$$

Molybdenum and life

Molybdenum is an essential element for all types of life, but it is only safe in tiny amounts. Molybdenum is an essential ingredient in an enzyme that is part of a natural process called the nitrogen cycle.

All forms of life need nitrogen to make proteins. Proteins are complicated chains made of mainly carbon, hydrogen, and oxygen atoms. Proteins can also be made of nitrogen and other elements. They are used to make cells, the building blocks of living bodies, and other substances important to life. Plants take nitrogen compounds from the soil through their roots. Molybdenum is needed to make sure nitrogen is in the soil in the first place.

The nitrogen cycle

Almost 80 percent of the air is nitrogen gas (N_2). The rest is mainly the oxygen (O_2) that animals, including humans,

These roots have tiny bags, or nodules, on them. These nodules are filled with bacteria. The bacteria use molybdenum to take nitrogen from the air and turn it into compounds that help plants grow.

breathe in. The main source of nitrogen on Earth is the atmosphere. However, nitrogen gas is very unreactive and does not form compounds easily.

Because plants cannot take it from the air, they must get their supply of nitrogen from compounds in the soil. These compounds are made by microscopic bacteria that take nitrogen gas from the air and react it with oxygen and hydrogen. This process is called "fixing," and the soil bacteria are called nitrogen-fixing bacteria.

Some plants have nitrogen-fixing bacteria living inside their roots. Plants like this are called legumes and include clover and pulses, such as lentils and beans. Farmers often grow legumes among other crops. This practice increases the amount of useful nitrogen-containing compounds in the soil and helps all the plants grow more quickly.

The role of molybdenum

Molybdenum is essential for the nitrogen cycle. Nitrogen-fixing bacteria use an enzyme to turn nitrogen gas in the air into nitrogen compounds. This enzyme contains molybdenum, which the bacteria take from the soil around them. If soil contains no molybdenum, the bacteria cannot make the nitrogen compounds that plants need. Farmers must add fertilizers—artificial nitrogen compounds—to make the soil fertile enough for plants to grow.

Animals eat plants to get the nitrogen compounds they need to make proteins and build up their bodies. Therefore molybdenum is important for all types of life.

In a healthy environment nitrogen is constantly recycled. When animals die, fungi (mushrooms and their relatives) and bacteria break down the dead bodies and return nitrogen compounds to the soil. Some of the bacteria also release nitrogen gas back into the air.

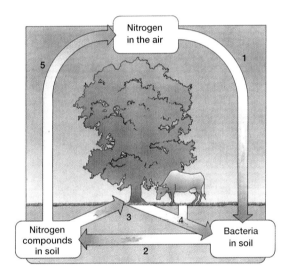

The nitrogen cycle is the way nitrogen atoms move between the atmosphere and living things. Part of the cycle involves a molybdenum-containing substance that converts nitrogen gas into nitrogen compounds. 1) Bacteria take nitrogen from the air. 2) They convert it into nitrogen compounds. 3) These are then taken up by plants and eaten by animals. 4) When living things die, more bacteria release the nitrogen compounds in the bodies back into the soil. 5) Some bacteria also release nitrogen gas into the air.

Periodic table

Everything in the universe is made from combinations of substances called elements. Elements are made of tiny atoms, which are too small to see. Atoms are the building blocks of matter.

The character of an atom depends on how many even tinier particles called protons there are in its center, or nucleus. An element's atomic number is the same as the number of its protons.

Scientists have found around 116 different elements. About 90 elements occur naturally on Earth. The rest have been made in experiments.

All these elements are set out on a chart called the periodic table. This lists all the elements in order according to their atomic number.

The elements at the left of the table are metals. Those at the right are nonmetals. Between the metals and the nonmetals are the metalloids, which sometimes act like metals and sometimes like nonmetals.

- On the left of the table are the alkali metals. These have just one outer electron.

- Metals get more reactive as you go down a group. The most reactive nonmetals are at the top of the table.

- On the right of the periodic table are the noble gases. These elements have full outer shells.

- The number of electrons orbiting the nucleus increases down each group.

- Elements in the same group have the same number of electrons in their outer shells.

- The transition metals are in the middle of the table, between Groups II and III.

Group I

Group II

Transition metals

Group I	Group II							
1 **H** Hydrogen 1								
3 **Li** Lithium 7	4 **Be** Beryllium 9							
11 **Na** Sodium 23	12 **Mg** Magnesium 24							
19 **K** Potassium 39	20 **Ca** Calcium 40	21 **Sc** Scandium 45	22 **Ti** Titanium 48	23 **V** Vanadium 51	24 **Cr** Chromium 52	25 **Mn** Manganese 55	26 **Fe** Iron 56	27 **Co** Cobalt 59
37 **Rb** Rubidium 85	38 **Sr** Strontium 88	39 **Y** Yttrium 89	40 **Zr** Zirconium 91	41 **Nb** Niobium 93	42 **Mo** Molybdenum 96	43 **Tc** Technetium (98)	44 **Ru** Ruthenium 101	45 **Rh** Rhodium 103
55 **Cs** Cesium 133	56 **Ba** Barium 137	71 **Lu** Lutetium 175	72 **Hf** Hafnium 179	73 **Ta** Tantalum 181	74 **W** Tungsten 184	75 **Re** Rhenium 186	76 **Os** Osmium 190	77 **Ir** Iridium 192
87 **Fr** Francium 223	88 **Ra** Radium 226	103 **Lr** Lawrencium (260)	104 **Rf** Rutherfordium (263)	105 **Db** Dubnium (268)	106 **Sg** Seaborgium (266)	107 **Bh** Bohrium (272)	108 **Hs** Hassium (277)	109 **Mt** Meitnerium (276)

Lanthanide elements

Actinide elements

57 **La** Lanthanum 39	58 **Ce** Cerium 140	59 **Pr** Praseodymium 141	60 **Nd** Neodymium 144	61 **Pm** Promethium (145)
89 **Ac** Actinium 227	90 **Th** Thorium 232	91 **Pa** Protactinium 231	92 **U** Uranium 238	93 **Np** Neptunium (237)

The horizontal rows are called periods. As you go across a period, the atomic number increases by one from each element to the next. The vertical columns are called groups. Elements get heavier as you go down a group. All the elements in a group have the same number of electrons in their outer shells. This means they react in similar ways.

The transition metals fall between Groups II and III. Their electron shells fill up in an unusual way. The lanthanide elements and the actinide elements are set apart from the main table to make it easier to read. All the lanthanide elements and the actinide elements are quite rare.

Molybdenum in the table

Molybdenum is in the second period of the transition metals. Like other transition metals, molybdenum atoms have empty spaces in both their two outermost electron shells. Electrons in both these shells take part in chemical reactions. This allows molybdenum atoms to form ions that have a variety of charges.

Metals

Metalloids (semimetals)

Nonmetals

42	Atomic (proton) number
Mo	Symbol
Molybdenum	Name
96	Atomic mass

			Group III	Group IV	Group V	Group VI	Group VII	Group VIII
								2 He Helium 4
			5 B Boron 11	6 C Carbon 12	7 N Nitrogen 14	8 O Oxygen 16	9 F Fluorine 19	10 Ne Neon 20
			13 Al Aluminum 27	14 Si Silicon 28	15 P Phosphorus 31	16 S Sulfur 32	17 Cl Chlorine 35	18 Ar Argon 40
28 Ni Nickel 59	29 Cu Copper 64	30 Zn Zinc 65	31 Ga Gallium 70	32 Ge Germanium 73	33 As Arsenic 75	34 Se Selenium 79	35 Br Bromine 80	36 Kr Krypton 84
46 Pd Palladium 106	47 Ag Silver 108	48 Cd Cadmium 112	49 In Indium 115	50 Sn Tin 119	51 Sb Antimony 122	52 Te Tellurium 128	53 I Iodine 127	54 Xe Xenon 131
78 Pt Platinum 195	79 Au Gold 197	80 Hg Mercury 201	81 Tl Thallium 204	82 Pb Lead 207	83 Bi Bismuth 209	84 Po Polonium (209)	85 At Astatine (210)	86 Rn Radon (222)
110 Ds Darmstadtium (281)	111 Rg Roentgenium (280)	112 Uub Ununbium (285)	113 Uut Ununtrium (284)	114 Uuq Ununquadium (289)	115 Uup Ununpentium (288)	116 Uuh Ununhexium (292)		

62 Sm Samarium 150	63 Eu Europium 152	64 Gd Gadolinium 157	65 Tb Terbium 159	66 Dy Dysprosium 163	67 Ho Holmium 165	68 Er Erbium 167	69 Tm Thulium 169	70 Yb Ytterbium 173
94 Pu Plutonium (244)	95 Am Americium (243)	96 Cm Curium (247)	97 Bk Berkelium (247)	98 Cf Californium (251)	99 Es Einsteinium (252)	100 Fm Fermium (257)	101 Md Mendelevium (258)	102 No Nobelium (259)

Chemical reactions

Chemical reactions are going on around us all the time. Some reactions involve just two substances, while others involve many more. But whenever a reaction takes place, at least one substance is changed.

In a chemical reaction, the atoms stay the same. But they join up in different combinations to form new molecules.

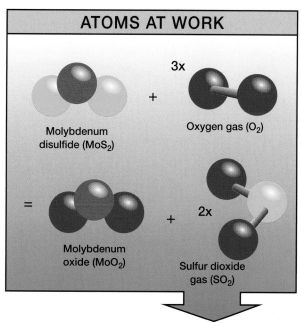

ATOMS AT WORK

Molybdenum disulfide (MoS_2)

3x
Oxygen gas (O_2)

=

Molybdenum oxide (MoO_2)

2x
Sulfur dioxide gas (SO_2)

The reaction that takes place can be written like this:
$$MoS_2 + 3O_2 \rightarrow MoO_2 + 2SO_2$$

A rocket engine's alloy nozzle gets very hot as the fuel burns. Adding molybdenum to the alloy gives the alloy a high melting point. The nozzle does not burn up when the engine is firing.

Writing an equation

Chemical reactions can be described by writing down the atoms and molecules before and after the reaction. Since the atoms stay the same, the number of atoms before the reaction will be the same as the number of atoms after. Chemists write the reaction as an equation. This shows what happens in the chemical reaction.

Making it balance

When the numbers of each atom on both sides of the equation are equal, the equation is balanced. If the numbers are not equal, something is wrong. The chemist adjusts the number of atoms involved until the equation balances.

Glossary

acid: An acid is a chemical that releases hydrogen ions easily during reactions.

atom: The smallest part of an element having all the properties of that element. Each atom is less than a millionth of an inch in diameter.

atomic mass number: The number of protons and neutrons in an atom.

atomic number: The number of protons in an atom.

bond: The attraction between two atoms or ions that holds them together.

compound: A substance made of atoms of two or more elements. The atoms are held together by chemical bonds.

corrosion: The eating away of a material by reaction with other chemicals, often oxygen and moisture in the air.

crystal: A solid consisting of a repeating pattern of atoms, ions, or molecules.

electron: A tiny particle with a negative charge. Inside atoms, electrons move around the nucleus in layers called shells.

element: A substance that is made from only one type of atom.

enzyme: A substance used by living things to control their life processes. Enzymes are made from proteins.

ion: An atom or a group of atoms that has lost or gained electrons to become electrically charged.

isotopes: Atoms of an element with the same number of protons and electrons, but different numbers of neutrons.

metal: An element on the left-hand side of the periodic table.

mineral: A compound or element as it is found in its natural form in Earth.

neutron: A tiny particle with no electrical charge. Neutrons are found in the nucleus of almost every atom.

nucleus: The dense structure at the center of an atom. Protons and neutrons are found inside the nucleus of an atom.

ore: A mineral that contains enough of a substance to make it useful for mining.

periodic table: A chart of all the chemical elements laid out in order of their atomic number.

protein: Substances used to build living bodies.

proton: A tiny particle with a positive charge. Protons are found in the nucleus.

radiation: Particles and rays produced when a radioactive element decays.

radioactivity: A property of certain unstable atoms that causes them to release radiation.

reaction: A process in which two or more elements or compounds combine to produce new substances.

transition metal: An element positioned in the middle of the periodic table. Transition metals have spaces in their outer electron shell and in the next shell in.

Index